The Roman Empire

Don Nardo

KidHaven Press, an imprint of Gale Group, Inc.
10911 Technology Place, San Diego, CA 92127

D0042498

Library of Congress Cataloging-in-Publication Data

Nardo, Don, 1947–
  The Roman empire / by Don Nardo.
    p. cm. — (History of the world)
  Includes bibliographical references.
  ISBN 0-7377-0775-5 (alk. paper)
    1. Rome—History—Empire, 30 B.C.–A.D. 476—Juvenile literature.
  2. Romans—Social life and customs—Juvenile literature. 3. Augustus,
  Emperor of Rome, 63 B.C.–A.D. 14—Juvenile literature. [1. Rome.]
  I. Title.
  DG270 .N37 2002
  937' .06—dc21

                                                        2001002247

Copyright 2002 by KidHaven Press, an imprint of Gale Group, Inc.
P.O. Box 289009, San Diego, California 92198-9009

No part of this book may be reproduced or used in any other form or
by any other means, electrical, mechanical, or otherwise, including, but
not limited to photocopy, recording, or any information storage and
retrieval system, without prior written permission from the publisher.

Printed in the U.S.A.

Contents

Chapter One

Augustus Creates a New Rome

The Roman Empire was one of the most powerful and influential empires in world history. At its height, all of the lands surrounding the Mediterranean Sea fell within its borders. What are now Italy, Greece, Turkey, Syria, Egypt, Spain, Libya, France, Britain—all these and more were part of the huge Roman realm. In all, it covered about 3.5 million square miles and was home to more than 100 million people.

The Empire began about 30 B.C., when Augustus, the first Roman emperor, came to power. However, in Augustus's day the city of Rome and the realm it ruled were already very old.

The Birth of the Empire

Rome grew on seven low hills located near the Tiber River, in western Italy. At first, Rome was ruled by

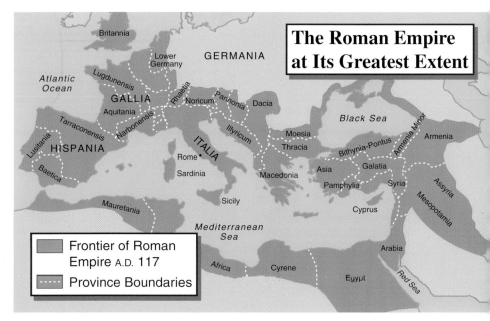

The Roman Empire at Its Greatest Extent

Britannia

GERMANIA

Lower Germany

Atlantic Ocean

Lugdunensis

GALLIA

Rhaetia

Noricum

Pannonia

Dacia

Aquitania

Black Sea

Tarraconensis

Narbonensis

Illyricum

Moesia

Armenia Minor

Armenia

Lusitania

HISPANIA

ITALIA

Rome

Thracia

Bithynia-Pontus

Baetica

Sardinia

Macedonia

Asia

Galatia

Syria

Assyria

Pamphylia

Mesopotamia

Mauretania

Sicily

Cyprus

Mediterranean Sea

Arabia

Frontier of Roman Empire A.D. 117

Province Boundaries

Africa

Cyrene

Egypt

Red Sea

kings. But about 509 B.C., the people threw out the last king and established the Roman Republic. It featured elected officials and a legislature called the Senate. In the next few hundred years the Roman Republic conquered all of its Italian neighbors. Then it sent its powerful armies beyond Italy. And by the first century B.C. (about two thousand years ago), it controlled almost the whole Mediterranean region.

But the Republic's great success had come at a price. In that same century, several destructive civil wars rocked Rome. One military general after another challenged the government and tried to gain power. The strongest of these generals, Julius Caesar, emerged the victor. He made himself dictator of Rome. But in 44 B.C., some senators stabbed Caesar to death. Another civil war erupted. This time, the winner was Caesar's adopted son, Octavian.

5

Roman senators attack and kill Julius Caesar, who had declared himself dictator.

Octavian became the most powerful man in Rome—more powerful than the Senate and other elected officials. The senators acknowledged this fact in 27 B.C. when they gave him a new name— Augustus. It meant "the revered one," that is, one who commands great respect and awe. Augustus's new government and realm based on one-man-rule became known as the Roman Empire.

Searching for a New Image

Augustus used his position for good rather than ill. He sincerely desired to help the Roman people put the death and destruction of the civil wars behind them. Like his father, Caesar, he envisioned a new Rome, one stronger and more splendid than ever before. Augustus also wanted to see the Roman realm enjoy the blessings of eternal peace and prosperity.

However, Augustus also knew that achieving these ambitious goals would not be easy. He would need the help of all Romans, including his former enemies. But what would be the best way to get that help?

Augustus asked the advice of his friend, Gaius Maecenas, a wealthy nobleman. Maecenas suggested that Augustus should create for himself the image of a simple man of the people. He should be a fair leader who respected the law, tradition, and religion and treated people with compassion. "If you perform all the actions which you would wish another man to perform if he were your ruler, you will succeed in all your endeavors," Maecenas said. "For how can men fail to regard you with affection as their father and their savior, when they see that you are both disciplined and principled in your life and that you show no arrogance and take no advantage of anyone?" [1]

Augustus ruled Rome for forty-five years.

The New Imperial Order

Augustus took Maecenas's advice. The new ruler never used the term emperor, though in reality he was the first of a long line of them. Instead, he called himself *princeps,* meaning "first citizen." He and his wife, Livia, rejected the lavish lifestyle of the wealthy and powerful and lived in a small, simply furnished house. Augustus humbly told the senators, "May I be privileged to build firm and lasting foundations for the government."[2] Indeed, the concept of building new and better things on the ruins of the past became the central policy of his long reign.

That policy was clearest in Augustus's public building programs. At the beginning of his reign, Rome was already a large and important city. But it was old, dirty, crowded, and ugly. It also suffered from many large fires that destroyed its poorly constructed apartment buildings, killing many people. In Augustus's view, the city was hardly a fitting centerpiece for his new empire. So he started a mighty burst of rebuilding. Augustus improved the city's appearance so much that he could later boast: "I found Rome built of bricks; I leave her clothed in marble."[3]

In the years that followed, Augustus created the most impressive city the world had yet seen. To make upkeep easier, he divided Rome into fourteen districts. Each had an administrator elected by the people of that district. The *princeps* ordered old roads to be repaired and new ones to be built. He put his friend and former admiral, Marcus Agrippa, in charge

This image depicts a modern artist's idea of what Rome's main square may have looked like in Augustus's time.

of repairing Rome's old **aqueducts,** or water lines, and creating new ones. To safeguard the city against fires, Augustus formed the world's first brigade of firemen—the *vigiles,* or "watchmen." He also created a police force for the city. His reign witnessed, in addition, the building of dozens of new temples honoring the Roman gods; the magnificent Theater of Marcellus (named after Augustus's nephew); and the beautiful *Ara Pacis,* the "Altar of Peace," dedicated to the Roman people.

A Role Well Played

All through his nearly forty-five-year reign, Augustus carried out his plan for building a better, more peaceful capital city and realm. But suddenly, in the year A.D. 14, he became ill. It soon became clear that he was dying, and his family and friends gathered by his bedside. "Have I played my part in the farce [play] of life well enough?" he asked. One of those present said that he had. "Since well I've played my part, then, gentle people" Augustus whispered, "pray applaud and send me with your thanks on my way."[4] Then, he feebly embraced Livia and died in her arms. The date was August 19, thirty-five days before his seventy-sixth birthday.

After his funeral, Augustus's remains were buried in this circular tomb near the Tiber River.

On hearing about Augustus's passing, the Roman nation grieved deeply. Over a hundred thousand people marched silently in his funeral procession. The mourners placed the coffin containing Augustus's body on a huge pile of wood and branches known as a pyre. As flames engulfed the coffin, a soldier released a lone eagle. Its ascent into the sky symbolized Augustus's spirit rising into heaven. Then, thousands of those watching wept openly as a choir of children sang a beautiful hymn in his honor.

Augustus was truly one of the most brilliant, accomplished, and beloved rulers in world history. Considering his record, he need not have worried about his role in "the farce of life." He had played it with exceeding skill. The question was whether the emperors who followed him would play their own parts as well. Only time would tell.

Chapter  Two

The Army and Public Games

Roman rulers, even popular ones like Augustus, always worried about the loyalty of their subjects. To help guard against rebellion, they developed tools for maintaining public order and the emperor's power. One of the those tools already existed at the time that Augustus formed the Empire. It was the Roman army. By his day, it was the strongest army in the world, yet he managed to make it even more efficient.

The second tool for maintaining order—public games—helped to control the masses by appeasing them. The idea was to keep the people busy and happy attending chariot races and gladiatorial fights. The rulers thought that happy, busy people would be less likely to protest or rebel. The Romans had staged such games in the past but the emperors greatly expanded them, both in size and number. These rulers even threw in an extra bonus; on a reg-

Thousands of lions, elephants, and other wild animals were killed in the Colosseum at events like this one.

ular basis, the government handed out free bread to the people. This policy of giving the people free entertainment and food became known as "bread and circuses." The term came from a critical remark by the Roman humorist Juvenal, who lived in the Empire's first century. "There's only two things that concern the common people," he said, "bread and circus games."[5]

Like a Well-Oiled Machine

The emperor's first means of control, the army, had already proved its worth by conquering the Mediterranean world. Over the centuries, the Roman military had undergone many improvements. And by Augustus's time, it worked like a well-oiled machine. Its soldiers were well disciplined, well trained, and often showed great courage. And they rarely tasted defeat. The first-century B.C. Jewish historian Josephus saw this army in action when it put down a rebellion that began in Palestine in A.D. 66. "No lack of discipline breaks up their ranks" he wrote.

> They never panic, [and] no toil wears them out. It would not be far from truth to call their drills bloodless battles and their battles bloody drills.[6]

Luckily for the emperors, only rarely did they have to use the army to maintain order in Rome and Italy, the Roman heartland. Most of the time, the soldiers guarded the Empire's borders, or they put down uprisings in the countries Rome had conquered.

Army Organization

The Roman army that Josephus witnessed in Palestine was largely Augustus's creation. He drastically reformed the military. And the first several emperors who succeeded him made few changes in his blueprint. First, he banned the draft, in which the government ordered men to serve. Instead, the soldiers in the new army were volunteers who saw serving as a career. Augustus also gave the soldiers large bonuses from time to time. And he provided them

A common military formation called a "tortoise" protected Roman soldiers from arrows and rocks.

with parcels of land as part of the pensions they received when they retired. These measures were designed to ensure loyalty to the emperor.

Augustus also reformed the military's structure. The early imperial army had about 154,000 troops in all. It broke down into twenty-eight units of about 5,500 men each. Each unit was known as a **legion.** Its commander, appointed by the emperor, was called a **legionary legate.** The officers directly under the legate were called **tribunes.** And under the tribunes were the **centurions,** each commanding a unit of eighty men, called a **century.**

The ordinary Roman soldiers, or **legionaries**, also formed still smaller units. Eight men made up a group (called a *contubernium*) similar to a platoon in a modern army. The eight men traveled, made camp,

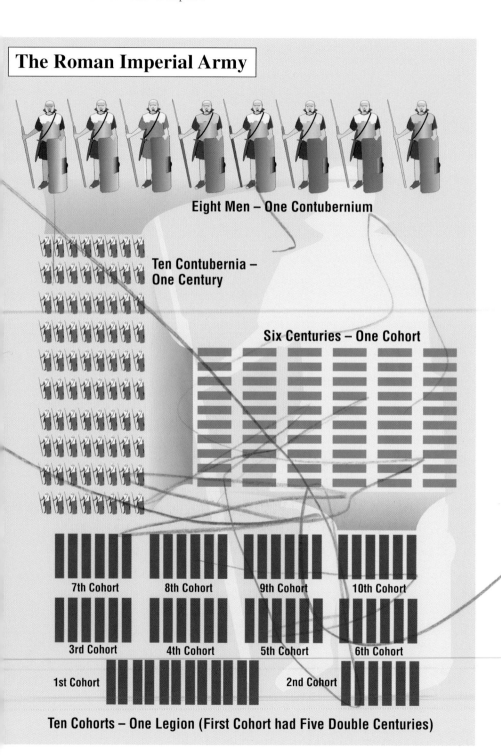

The Roman Imperial Army

Eight Men – One Contubernium

**Ten Contubernia –
One Century**

Six Centuries – One Cohort

7th Cohort   8th Cohort   9th Cohort   10th Cohort

3rd Cohort   4th Cohort   5th Cohort   6th Cohort

1st Cohort   2nd Cohort

Ten Cohorts – One Legion (First Cohort had Five Double Centuries)

and ate together. They also shared the same tent. From top to bottom, the imperial army was a model of organization and efficiency. That is one reason that it was such a powerful tool in the hands of the emperors.

Chariot Races and Gladiatorial Combats

The other tool the emperors employed to maintain order—the public games—consisted of four general types. The first and perhaps most popular was chariot racing. The drivers often became fan favorites, like popular football and basketball stars today. Also like modern sports stars, charioteers who won regularly became rich from their earnings. As Juvenal put it, "You'll find that a hundred lawyers scarcely make more than a single charioteer."[7] One successful and famous charioteer, Calpurnianus, won 1,127 victories. Several of these paid him a sum equal to forty times the annual wage of an average Roman soldier, or more!

Calpurnianus and his fellow charioteers raced in long, oval-shaped structures known as **circuses**. The largest was the Circus Maximus, or "Great Circus," in Rome. It was over a third of a mile long and could seat 150,000 or more spectators. A typical race consisted of seven laps around the inside of the circus, a total of about two and a half miles. These races were exciting, but they were also dangerous. Sometimes chariots crashed into one another, creating a mass of twisted debris and broken bones.

Although charioteers sometimes died on the job, far fewer racers died than gladiators. The gladiatorial

Charioteers vie for the lead during a race in the great Circus Maximus. Crashes on the track could be deadly.

combats took place in round, stadium-like structures called **amphitheaters.** The largest and most famous was the Colosseum, in Rome. First, the fighters marched into the arena in a sort of parade. Some wore heavy metal armor and wielded swords and shields. Others had no armor and carried nets and spears. Still others rode on horses or chariots. When the parade ended, all of them raised their weapons to the emperor (or highest official present) and shouted, "We who are about to die salute you!"

Then the first pair fought. Sometimes one gladiator killed the other. Another common outcome was when one man went down wounded. He raised one finger, an appeal for mercy from the emperor and crowd. Sometimes they called for death, but just as often they spared the wounded man. Occasionally, a match ended in a draw and the fighters exited the arena together.

Animal Hunts and Naval Battles

Gladiators did not always kill other gladiators. Sometimes they executed convicted criminals in the arena. Criminals also took part in two other popular public games. One was the so-called "animal hunt." Sometimes one or more half-starved lions or bears attacked and ate a condemned person. But more often, the hunts consisted of combats between wild animals and trained fighters similar to gladiators.

In still another kind of public game, almost *all* the participants were criminals, slaves, or war captives. They acted as crews on opposing ships in staged naval battles. Such spectacles took place in lakes or large specially dug basins. As crowds watched, the ships rammed one another and the crewmen fought to the death. Augustus staged one of the most impressive naval spectacles ever. He later bragged that he

> had the site excavated [dug up] 1,800 feet in length and 1,200 feet in width. Thirty ships with rams on their fronts and a great number of smaller vessels engaged in combat. On board these fleets there were about 3,000 fighters.[8]

Augustus had good reason to brag. He set a standard for such games that his successors tried to match or surpass. Only a few managed to do so.

Chapter Three

Overseers of the Realm

The success of any great nation or empire depends in large degree on the quality of its leaders. In the 506 years of the Roman Empire's existence, about ninety-five men sat on its throne as emperor. Some, like Augustus, were strong, just, and skilled rulers. They accomplished much for Rome. Others were unjust, brutal, inept, dishonest, or weak. That Rome lasted so long is a tribute to the good emperors. For centuries, their constructive deeds and efforts often made up for the *de-*structive effects of the bad emperors.

A Long Series of Good Rulers

Good emperors far outnumbered bad ones in the Empire's early years. Most of the eighteen overseers of the realm in its first two centuries were fair-minded and skilled at leading. They continued to expand and beautify the capital city, Rome. And they often brought roads, aqueducts, laws, schools, commerce, and other aspects of civilization to undeveloped areas. This period lasted from about 30 B.C. to A.D. 180. Because the Empire enjoyed relative peace and widespread prosperity, it became known as the *Pax Romana,* or "Roman Peace." Times were so good for so many people under Roman rule that a Greek writer observed:

Every place is full of gymnasiums, fountains, gateways, temples, shops, and schools. Only

Statues depict three of the five good emperors: Marcus Aurelius (left), Trajan (middle), and Hadrian.

those outside the Empire are to be pitied for losing such blessings. You [i.e., Rome] have surveyed the whole world and civilized it all with system and order.[9]

Augustus did much to create this new order, and many of his immediate successors carried on his work. One of these was Vespasian, who ruled from 69–79. Vespasian was a very popular emperor, known for being honest, hardworking, and wise. He was also a great builder. His most famous building project was the Colosseum, Rome's largest arena. Greatly impressing his subjects, he carted away the first load of dirt dug from the construction site. The five emperors who ruled from 96 to 180 were just as honest and hardworking as Vespasian. As a result, they became known as the "five good emperors." Under them, the Empire reached its height of prosperity and splendor.

Two Infamous Tyrants

Only a few emperors of the *Pax Romana* era deserve to be called bad. One, Caligula (37–41), was Augustus's great-grandson. But

Vespasian and his son, Titus, study a model of the Colosseum.

he was nothing like Augustus. Cruel and mentally unbalanced, Caligula demanded that his subjects worship him like a god. In addition, he imposed unfair taxes on the people and spent much of the money on himself. In less than two years, for example, he spent the entire treasury surplus that earlier emperors had built up. Along with his spending on public games, Caligula built himself a palace and huge pleasure barges equipped with baths, banquet halls, and gardens. Hatred for him became so great that his own bodyguards finally killed him.

Nero (51–68) was another tyrant. He murdered his own mother and both of his wives. He also amused himself by disguising himself and mugging innocent people. According to the Roman historian Suetonius:

> As soon as night fell, he would put on a cap or a wig and prowl the streets in search of mischief. One of his games was to attack men on their way home from dinner, stab them if they offered resistance, and then drop their bodies down the sewers.[10]

Like Caligula, Nero became widely hated. Fed up, several generals and other high-ranking people turned on him. Fearing assassination, he took his own life.

Luckily, most of Caligula's and Nero's aides were able administrators. So the Empire continued to run smoothly and remained prosperous during the reigns of these emperors.

A Long Series of Bad Rulers

However, the Empire was not so lucky in the years following the *Pax Romana*. That era ended when the last of the five good emperors, Marcus Aurelius, died in 180. His successor, his son Commodus (180–192), was a selfish, brutal man. He cared little about the welfare of the Roman people. Like Caligula and Nero, he spent large sums of public money on his own pleasures. Commodus also executed hundreds of people whom he suspected of disloyalty to him. Nearly everyone came to hate him and an assassin finally ended his life and reign.

At this point, Rome needed several good, strong emperors to follow Commodus. Instead, a long series of ambitious, weak, brutal, or inept rulers occupied the throne. In addition to poor leadership, Rome suddenly began to experience other serious problems. Poverty sharply increased. Also, Germanic tribes living beyond the Empire's northern borders grew uneasy and began attacking Roman cities. While trying to fend them off, some Roman generals wasted men and resources by fighting among themselves. These factors combined to make life in the Empire increasingly dangerous, miserable, and uncertain.

Recovery Under Some Strong Emperors

The Roman Empire appeared to be doomed. But then, beginning in A.D. 268, a series of strong military generals sat on Rome's throne. Claudius II, Aurelian, Carus, and a few others managed to restore order.

Roman soldiers battle so-called barbarians from northern Europe during the third century.

The last of this group, Diocletian (284–305), proved to be the most capable, forceful leader since Marcus Aurelius. Diocletian breathed new life into the ailing realm. He rebuilt the army, which had suffered crippling losses in recent years. He also made the provinces smaller and easier to manage.

More important, Diocletian felt that the Empire was too large for one man to administer well. So he divided up the leadership. He ruled the realm's eastern portion from Nicomedia, in Asia Minor (what is now Turkey). He appointed another capable man, Maximian (286–305), to rule the western portion.

Diocletian was not as wise and just as he was strong and efficient. He and his assistant, Galerius, began to attack Roman Christians. Christianity had appeared during the *Pax Romana,* and over the years, the Christians had increased in number. But many non-Christian Romans mistakenly thought that the Christians posed a threat to law and order. Trying to remove this danger, Diocletian and Galerius closed Christian churches. They also threw many Christian leaders into prison. One eyewitness wrote, "Everywhere the prisons were filled with Christians, so that there was no longer any room left for real criminals."[11]

The Final Decline and Fall

This attempt to slow the growth of Christianity failed. Another emperor, Constantine I (306–337), believed that the Christian god had helped him win a major battle. So he befriended the Christians. He erected

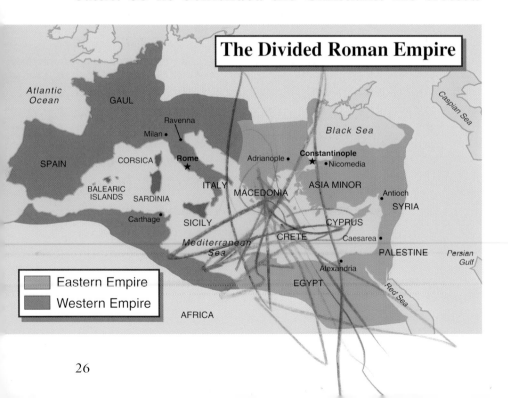

The Divided Roman Empire

Atlantic Ocean

GAUL

Ravenna

Milan

Black Sea

SPAIN

CORSICA

Rome

Adrianople

Constantinople

Nicomedia

BALEARIC ISLANDS

SARDINIA

ITALY

MACEDONIA

ASIA MINOR

Antioch

SYRIA

Carthage

SICILY

CYPRUS

Mediterranean Sea

CRETE

Caesarea

PALESTINE

Persian Gulf

Alexandria

EGYPT

Red Sea

Caspian Sea

Eastern Empire

Western Empire

AFRICA

A lion menaces a group of Christians in a Roman arena.

hundreds of Christian churches. And he became the first emperor to convert to the faith. Thereafter, all but one of the emperors were Christians.

Though Constantine was a great builder and fair ruler, most of the emperors who followed him were less effective. Beginning about 375, they faced a new wave of foreign invasions. These were much larger than those of the previous century. This time, the emperors and their armies were unable to stop the realm's decline. Many weak emperors lost important Roman territories, including Britain, Spain, and much of what is now France. Finally, all that was left was Italy and small portions of some nearby provinces. The last emperor was Romulus Augustulus (475–476). A foreign general forced this weak, inexperienced young man off the throne in 476. Later ages came to see this as the fall of the Roman Empire.

Chapter Four

Rediscovering the Ancient Romans

After the Empire fell, Rome and other Italian cities continued to exist. People still went about their daily lives, but over time they no longer saw themselves as Romans. As the centuries rolled on, they dismantled many of the palaces and other large Roman buildings and used the stones to build more modest structures. Most of the rest of the old monuments were abandoned and fell into decay.

People in later ages looked at the ruined Colosseum and other Roman remains and wondered when they had been built. Also, why and how were they built? And what was the history of the builders themselves? The answers to these questions seemed shrouded in darkness.

Fortunately, some small rays of light illuminated the darkness during the Renaissance. In that era, last-

ing from the early 1300s to the late 1500s, the Italians and other Europeans expressed an intense interest in art and literature. They also rediscovered many ancient Roman writings, including the works of Roman poets. And they learned much about Roman history.

But many questions remained about the Romans. To answer such questions properly, people needed to preserve and study the existing Roman ruins; they also needed to dig up and examine thousands more that still lay buried. But for a long time no one had

A Renaissance artist depicts Aeneas, the mythical founder of the Roman race.

the money, interest, or skill to attempt such huge and difficult projects. A new science devoted to such work did not emerge until the 1700s and 1800s.

Buried Treasures Come to Light

That new science was **archaeology,** the careful recovery and study of past civilizations. It began in southwestern Italy not far from Mt. Vesuvius, a volcano located near the Bay of Naples. Two thousand years ago, several small Roman towns existed on the volcano's lower slopes. The most important were Pompeii and Herculaneum (the "city of Hercules"). The larger of the two, Pompeii, was a bustling community. It boasted some twenty thousand inhabi-

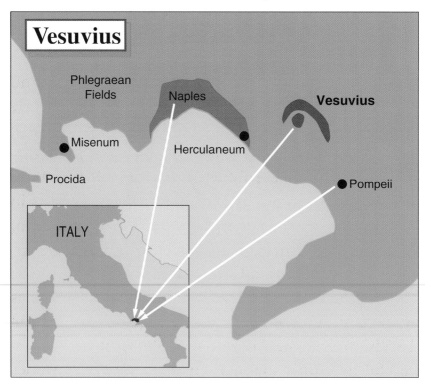

tants, many prosperous shops and restaurants, and the Roman Empire's first all-stone amphitheater. Surrounding the towns were hundreds of busy farms and vineyards, all taking advantage of the rich volcanic soil.

That quaint, attractive scene ended abruptly and forever on August 24, in the year A.D. 79. Without warning, Mt. Vesuvius blew its top. Ashes and blackened stones fell "hot and thick," an eyewitness later recorded.

> On Mt. Vesuvius, broad sheets of fire and leaping flames blazed at several points. The buildings [in the towns] rocked with violent shocks, and seemed to be swaying to and fro as if they were torn from their foundations.[12]

The eruption completely buried Pompeii and Herculaneum, erasing them from the map. Nearly seventeen centuries went by. And during all these years, the towns and their contents rested undisturbed beneath the rubble. In the early 1700s, local Italians began to dig up statues and other artifacts in the area. Their methods were crude and random, however. Also, their goal was not knowledge but to find art treasures to adorn their houses and gardens.

Luckily, though, when word of these discoveries spread, some scholars became interested. In the 1760s, they began digging at Pompeii in a more careful, scientific manner. In turn, their discoveries

The ruins of Pompeii, with the city's theater at left. Mt. Vesuvius looms in the distance.

ignited widespread interest in learning how the ancient Romans lived. The tools and methods employed by these scholars improved over time. And as the buried towns began to emerge from the ashes, similar digs began at other ancient Roman sites.

A Slice of Life Captured

Today, more than three-quarters of Pompeii has been uncovered. The task of unearthing the rest of the town continues. In 1991, the Italian government gave archaeologists $23 million for the project, which will go on well into the twenty-first century.

The remains of Pompeii are like a time capsule. The ash that buried it captured a slice of everyday Roman life and preserved it for all times. Among the finds: the amphitheater, with the names of its builders still carved on its front; living quarters for the gladiators who fought there; streets lined with shops and snack bars; houses, along with their furniture, oil lamps, kitchen pots and pans, wall paintings, and the jewelry and other personal items of the occupants.

Among the more revealing discoveries at Pompeii are its bakeries. The town may have had as many as thirty in all. Their mills for grinding grain and ovens for baking bread are often intact or nearly so. In one

A drawing of Roman bakers at work is based on the ruins of bakeries found at Pompeii.

such shop, the so-called "bakery of Modestus," diggers made an amazing find. Eighty-one loaves of bread still rested in the ovens where the bakers left them when they fled the volcano's wrath. Archaeologists even found one bakery whose owner made his own brand of dog biscuits.

The Romans Revealed from Their Bones

Some equally exciting discoveries have been made at the other buried city—Herculaneum. In 1980, Italian archaeologist Giuseppe Maggi found more than 150 complete skeletons. They lay near the town's waterfront and docks. So Maggi reasoned that the people were trying to escape the eruption by boat. Unfortunately for them, a blast of hot, poisonous

The solidified remains of a resident of Pompeii, buried beneath volcanic ash over nineteen centuries ago.

gases smothered them to death. But fortunately for later ages, volcanic debris buried their bodies and preserved their remains.

The reason this discovery is so important is that prior to it few intact skeletons of Romans had ever been found. This is because most Romans cremated (burned), rather than buried, their dead. Studies of the human remains Maggi found have revealed the ages of the victims. Examinations of their teeth show how many cavities they had. The bones of some skeletons have scars showing that their owners performed unusually heavy work; so scholars concluded that these were slaves. Among the remains was the only complete skeleton of a Roman soldier ever found. It has a battle wound on the left thigh. And three teeth are missing, probably knocked out in a fight.

More than Just a Place

Meanwhile, across Italy and other parts of Europe, efforts to preserve existing Roman ruins are ongoing. Perhaps the most famous example is the Colosseum. Over the ages, grass and trees grew up inside the unused structure, and earthquakes caused some of its walls to collapse. The English poet Percy Bysshe Shelley visited the Colosseum in 1818 and wrote: "It is overgrown by wild olive trees and threaded by little paths, which wind among its ruined stairs."[13]

The Colosseum's rescue and preservation began in 1825, when workmen braced the remaining walls

The surviving ruins of the Colosseum are stunning proof that the Romans were the greatest builders of the ancient world.

against further collapse. In 1870, they cleared away all the weeds from the interior, and restoration efforts have gone on ever since. The latest and most expensive began in 1992 and is ongoing. Tens of thousands of tourists visit the Colosseum every year and stand within its silent arena. Some try to picture the thousands of people and animals who died there long ago as crowds roared.

Indeed, it must never be forgotten that people of flesh and blood once inhabited this and other Roman ruins. The Roman Empire was much more than a mere thing or place. More than anything else, it was a group of human beings who lived, and loved, and dreamed, just as people do today.

Notes

Chapter One: Augustus Creates a New Rome

1. Quoted in Dio Cassius, *Roman History: The Reign of Augustus*. Trans. Ian Scott-Kilvert. New York: Penguin Books, 1987, p. 123.
2. Quoted in Suetonius, *The Twelve Caesars*. Trans. Robert Graves. Rev. Michael Grant. New York: Penguin Books, 1979, p. 69.
3. Quoted in Suetonius, *Twelve Caesars,* p. 69.
4. Quoted in Suetonius, *Twelve Caesars,* p. 110.

Chapter Two: The Army and Public Games

5. Juvenal, *Satires,* published as *Juvenal: The Sixteen Satires*. Trans. Peter Green. New York: Penguin Books, 1974, p. 207.
6. Josephus, *The Jewish War*. Trans. G. A. Williamson. Rev. E. Mary Smallwood. New York: Penguin Books, 1970 and 1981, pp. 194–95.
7. Juvenal, *Satires,* p. 167.
8. Augustus, *Res Gestae,* in Naphtali Lewis and Meyer Reinhold, eds., *Roman Civilization, Sourcebook II: The Empire*. New York: Harper and Row, 1966, p. 16.

Chapter Three: Overseers of the Realm

9. Aelius Aristides, *Roman Panegyric,* quoted in Lewis and Reinhold, *Roman Civilization, Sourcebook II,* p. 138.

10. Suetonius, *Twelve Caesars,* p.227.
11. Eusebius, *Ecclesiastical History,* quoted in Lewis and Reinhold, *Roman Civilization, Sourcebook II,* pp. 599–600.

Chapter Four: Rediscovering the Ancient Romans
12. Pliny the Younger, *Letters,* in *The Letters of the Younger Pliny.* Trans. Betty Radice. New York: Penguin Books, 1969, pp. 167–68.
13. Quoted in Peter Quennell, *The Colosseum.* New York: Newsweek Book Division, 1971, p. 120.

Glossary

amphitheater: A round, roofless wooden or stone structure in which the ancient Romans staged gladiatorial combats and wild animal shows.

aqueduct: A channel for carrying water to a town or other human habitation.

archaeology: The careful recovery and study of past civilizations.

centurion: In the Roman army, the commander of a century.

century: In the Roman army, a unit originally consisting of one hundred and later eighty soldiers.

circus: A long, roofless structure in which the Romans staged chariot races.

contubernium: A unit in the Roman army of eight men who shared the same tent. (Plural: ***contubernia***).

legion: In the army of the early Roman empire, a unit of about 5000 to 5500 soldiers.

legionary: An ordinary Roman soldier.

legionary legate: The commander of a Roman army legion.

Pax Romana: Latin for "Roman Peace," referring to the prosperous period lasting from about 30 B.C. to about A.D. 180.

princeps: Latin for "first citizen."

tribune: In the Roman army, an officer who was second in command, ranked directly under the legionary legate.

vigiles: Latin for "watchmen," the fire-fighters of ancient Rome.

For Further Exploration

Isaac Asimov, *The Roman Empire*. Boston: Houghton Mifflin, 1967. An excellent overview of the main events of the Empire; so precise and clearly written that even very basic readers will benefit.

Lionel Casson, *Daily Life in Ancient Rome*. New York: American Heritage Publishing, 1975. A well-written presentation of how the Romans lived: their homes, streets, entertainment, foods, theaters, religion, slaves, marriage customs, and more.

Peter Connolly, *Greece and Rome at War*. London: Macdonald, 1981. A very informative and useful book that is highly recommended for advanced or ambitious young readers, or even just for the many stunning color illustrations (by Connolly himself).

———, *Pompeii*. New York: Oxford University Press, 1994. An excellent introduction to how archaeologists dug up this ancient Roman town. Connolly's many color illustrations are, as usual, breathtakingly beautiful.

Louise James, *How We Know About the Romans*. New York: Peter Bedrick Books, 1997. An excellent book that tells how scholars learn about ancient Rome by digging up its ruins, artworks, and other artifacts.

Anthony Marks and Graham Tingay, *The Romans.* London: Usborne Publishing, 1990. An excellent summary of the main aspects of Roman history, life, and art, supported by hundreds of beautiful and accurate drawings reconstructing Roman times.

Don Nardo, *The Roman Republic* and *The Roman Empire,* both San Diego: Lucent Books, 1994; *The Age of Augustus.* San Diego: Lucent Books, 1996; *Greek and Roman Mythology* and *Life in Ancient Rome,* both San Diego: Lucent Books, 1997; *Life of a Roman Slave.* San Diego: Lucent Books, 1998; and *The Ancient Romans.* San Diego: Lucent Books, 2000. These comprehensive but easy-to-read volumes provide an overview of Roman life and history for junior high and high school readers (as well as ambitious younger readers).

Jonathan Rutland, *See Inside a Roman Town.* New York: Barnes and Noble, 1986. A very attractively illustrated introduction to some major concepts of Roman civilization for basic readers.

Judith Simpson, *Ancient Rome.* New York: Time-Life Books, 1997. This is one of the latest entries in Time-Life's library of picture books about the ancient world. It is beautifully illustrated with attractive and appropriate photographs and paintings. The general but well-written text is aimed at intermediate young readers.

Chester G. Starr, *The Ancient Romans.* New York: Oxford University Press, 1971. A clearly written survey of Roman history, featuring several interesting sidebars on such subjects as the Etruscans, Roman law, and the Roman army. Written for intermediate and advanced young readers.

Index

Picture Credits

Cover photo: Manchester City Arts Galleries, UK/ Bridgeman Art Library

© Araldo de Luca/CORBIS, 7

© Archivo Icongrafico, S.A./CORBIS, 21 (all)

© Charles and Josette Lenars/CORBIS, 15

© National Gallery Collection; By kind permission of the Trustees of the National Gallery, London/ CORBIS, 29

© Richard Glover/CORBIS, 36

© Roger Ressmeyer/CORBIS, 32, 34

© Ruggero Vanni/CORBIS, 10

Hulton-Getty, 13

Chris Jouan, 16

North Wind Picture Archives, 6, 9, 18, 22, 25, 27, 33

Martha Schierholtz, 5, 26, 30

About the Author

A historian and award-winning writer, Don Nardo has written or edited numerous books about the ancient world. Among these are *Life of a Roman Slave*, *Roman Roads and Aqueducts*, *Greek and Roman Sport*, and Greenhaven Press's massive *Complete History of Ancient Greece* and *A–Z Encyclopedia of Ancient Rome*. He lives with his wife, Christine, in Massachusetts.